December, 1975
Robbie –
– From –
Missy & Chrissy

WHAT BUS CROSSED THE OCEAN?

ON WHICH SIDE OF A CHURCH DOES A TREE GROW?

WHAT TEN-LETTER
WORD STARTS WITH
GAS?

WHAT IS AT THE
END OF DUMBO?

Mickey Mouse's Riddle Book

Random House New York

Library of Congress Cataloging in Publication Data
Mickey Mouse's riddle book.
A collection of riddles for young readers illustrated with Disney characters.
1. Riddles—Juvenile literature.   [1. Riddles]
PN6371.5.M5   398.6   72-5165   ISBN 0-394-82521-7   ISBN 0-394-92521-1 (lib. bdg.)
Manufactured in the United States of America

What three-letter word
is a mousetrap?

Cat!

Why does a giraffe eat so little?

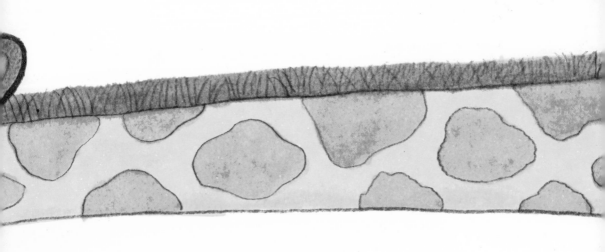

Because a little goes a long way.

If two is company,

and three is a crowd . . .

what are four,

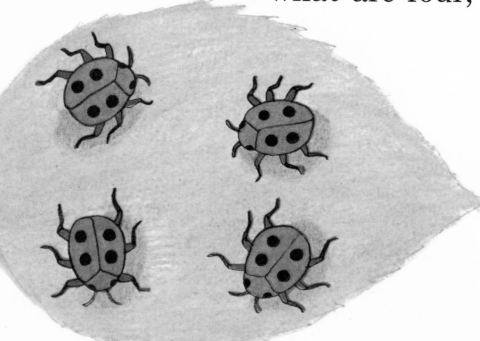

and five?

NINE!

When are cooks mean?

When they beat the eggs.

And whip the cream.

What kind of shoes are
made of banana skins?

Slippers!

If twenty dogs run after one dog,
what time is it?

Twenty after one.

What did the rug say to the floor?

"Don't move,
I have you covered."

Which month
has 28 days in it?

All months have.

Who always goes to sleep with his shoes on?

A horse.

What has the head of a cat, the tail
of a cat—and is not a cat?

A kitten.

Why do you salute a refrigerator?

Because it is General Electric.

What bus crossed the ocean?

Columbus.

Where was Mickey Mouse when the lights went out?

In the dark.

Why does a spider make a good baseball player?

Because he catches flies.

What has many eyes and never cries?

A potato.

What dog keeps the best time?

A watch dog.

What is full of holes,
but holds water?

A sponge.

What did one wall
say to another?

"Meet you at the corner."

When is a sheep dog
most likely to go into a house?

When the door is open.

How do you look at a hippo's teeth?

Very carefully.

What is the difference between Donald Duck and an umbrella?

You can shut an umbrella up.

Why are fish so smart?

Because they travel in schools.

A butcher is six feet tall,
and wears a size twelve shoe.
What does he weigh?

Meat, of course.

What do you call a cat
who drinks lemonade?

A sourpuss.

What is black and white,
and has sixteen wheels?

A zebra on roller skates.

What ten-letter word
starts with *GAS?*

AUTOMOBILE!

On which side
of a church
does a tree grow?

On the outside.

When are
mice and rats
unhappy?

When it is raining
cats and dogs.

What did the dirt say when it rained?

If this keeps up my name is mud!

Why is the
Statue of Liberty
standing in
New York harbor?

Because she can't sit down.

What is at
the end of Dumbo?

The letter O.

What are the last two words in this book?

The end.